D0521459

Making Wreaths

Making Wreaths

Barbara Radcliffe Rogers

FRIEDMAN/FAIRFAX PUBLISHERS

A FRIEDMAN/FAIRFAX BOOK

Copyright © 1993 by Michael Friedman Publishing Group, Inc.

All rights reserved. No part of this publication may be reproduced, stored in a retrieval system, or transmitted, in any form or by any means, electronic, mechanical, photocopying, recording, or otherwise, without the prior written permission of the publisher.

ISBN 1-56799-026-6

Editor: Sharyn Rosart
Art Director: Jeff Batzli
Designer: Lynne Yeamans
Photography Editor: Christopher C. Bain
Illustrator: Madeline Sorel

Typeset by The Interface Group, Inc.
Color separations by Kwong Ming Graphicprint Co.
Printed and bound in China by Leefung-Asco Printers Ltd.

For bulk purchases and special sales, please contact:
Friedman/Fairfax Publishers
15 West 26 Street
New York, NY 10010
(212) 685-6610 FAX (212) 685-1307

DEDICATION

To my friend Maria Sibley, with happy memories of the hours we've spent making wreaths together.

AUTHOR'S ACKNOWLEDGMENTS

It is appropriate that writing a book about wreaths, which have long symbolized the welcoming circle of friendship, should involve so many friends. Many thanks to my youngest neighbor, Aram Gurian, whose generous gifts of the beautiful things he's found growing in his woods and fields have brightened both my wreaths and my days.

My thanks to Frank Sibley for rescuing my entire crop of Sweet Annie from the frost (and storing it in his barn); to Michael Gurian for the multitude of supplies that his workshop always seems to have when I'm desperate; to my brother-in-law Doug Rogers, whose wreaths have decorated our home for years; and to my mother, Dee Radcliffe, who finds room in her tiny garden to grow sprawling tansy and artemisia for my projects.

Making the wreaths was only the beginning; finding a place in which to show them at their best was equally important. For this, my friends Pat and Glynn Wells offered their two-century-old Hancock Inn in Hancock, New Hampshire, as a setting for all the photography. Their hospitality, not to mention the outstanding meals in the inn's dining room, made the whole experience a pleasure.

And a final word of thanks to my family, each of whom has taken part in growing the flowers, gathering the materials, and making the wreaths. It is only with their incalculable help that this and my other books have been possible.

CONTENTS

INTRODUCTION
page 9

CHAPTER ONE:
MATERIALS AND TECHNIQUES
page 13

Bases, Rings
and Frames
page 14

Tools and Supplies
page 16

Ribbons and Bows
page 18

Making Bows
for Wreaths
page 20

Tied Bows
page 21

Wire Wrapped Bows
page 22

Ribbon Wrapped
Bows
page 24

Attaching Bows
page 25

CHAPTER TWO:
THE WREATH-MAKER'S GARDEN
page 27

Flowers
page 29

Herbs
page 32

Vegetables
page 35

CHAPTER THREE:
EVERGREEN WREATHS
page 37

A Basic
Evergreen
Wreath
page 41

Decorating
an Evergreen
Wreath
page 44

CHAPTER FOUR:
FRESH PLANT WREATHS
page 47

A Fresh Artemisia
Wreath Base
page 51

A Living Wreath
of Thyme
page 55

A Living Wreath
of Partridgeberries
page 57

CHAPTER FIVE:
VINE WREATHS
page 59

A Ribboned
Vine Wreath
page 63

A Vine Wreath
with Flowers
page 67

Vine Terra-Cotta
Wreath
page 69

CHAPTER SIX:
CONE AND SEED
WREATHS
page 71

Attaching Wires
to Cones
page 74

Creating
Cone Flowers
page 74

A Cone Wreath
page 77

A Miniature
Cone
Wreath
page 81

An Austrian
Cone
Wreath
page 83

CHAPTER SEVEN:
CORNHUSK
AND
RAFFIA
WREATHS
page 85

A Cornhusk
Wreath
page 89

A Fringed
Cornhusk
Wreath
page 93

Creating
Cornhusk
Flowers
page 94

Making
a Cornhusk
Bow
page 95

A Raffia
Wreath
page 97

CHAPTER EIGHT:
DRIED FLOWER
AND
HERB WREATHS
page 101

Wiring Stems
of Dried Plants
page 104

A Wreath of
Sweet Annie and
Autumn Flowers
page 107

An Edwardian
Wreath of
Silver Artemisia
page 109

Braided Hemp
Kitchen Wreath
page 113

A Harvest Circle
of Grain
page 115

A Large
Everlasting
Wreath
page 117

A Kitchen Wreath
of Dried Herbs
page 121

SOURCES
page 125

INDEX
page 126

Nature abounds with materials for beautiful wreaths, from the cones, nuts, and seed pods of the woodlands to the grasses and weeds of the field.

© Sharon Guynup

INTRODUCTION

*Since ancient times the wreath—a simple circle of leaves, boughs, or flowers
—has served as a symbol of honor, hospitality, faith, or celebration. The
Greeks crowned their victors with wreaths of laurel leaves, the origin of the
expression "to rest on his laurels." Hawaiians to this day welcome guests and
celebrate joyous occasions with leis, circular garlands of fresh flowers. A
wreath with candles heralds the approach of Christmas and wreaths hang on
the door to welcome guests throughout the holiday season.*

*A wreath on the door is by no means limited to the winter holidays. A
wreath of cornhusks or golden wheat celebrates the harvest, while one of
flowers welcomes guests in spring and summer.*

*Pinecones, seedpods and seed heads, dried flowers, nuts, vines, grasses,
herbs, whole spices, clay, fabric, cane, rope, and a variety of other materials
can become wreaths. The basic methods of working with evergreen boughs,
herbs, and dried flowers are much the same, so learning wreath making is
easy. Any wreath in this book can be mastered in an evening.*

For those too busy to construct a wreath from scratch, there are many types of bases available for trimming, making it possible to enjoy the creative fun of decorating without the more time-consuming construction.

The materials are usually inexpensive, and many are free for those with woods and fields. Florist shops and craft-supply stores carry the basic frames and wires, with most other materials and tools commonly available.

Once the basic skills are yours, ideas will come from everywhere. A craft show might inspire you to decorate a green wreath with small hand-carved wooden birds and animals. Christmas tree ornaments, treasures from the garden, even discarded jewelry can be used creatively in wreaths. Soon the only limitation to your wreath making and designing will be the wall, door, and window space for hanging your creations.

© Derek Fell

The vegetable garden provided the brilliant color of this dried pepper wreath at Lambshead Ranch in Texas.

CHAPTER ONE

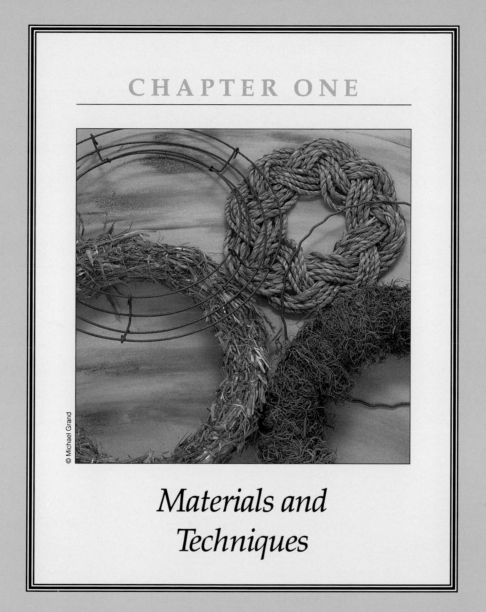

© Michael Grand

Materials and Techniques

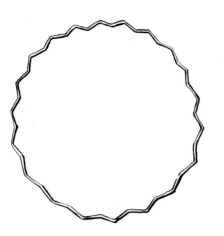

A crinkle-wire wreath frame

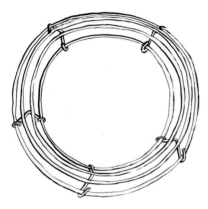

A double-wire wreath frame

A straw wreath base

As in any craft, wreath making is easier when you use the right tools and materials. Fortunately, these are few, inexpensive, and readily available from craft and hobby shops or florists. • While it is possible to make wreaths on frames made of bent wire clothes hangers, these are hard to work with and often disappointing. For the modest cost of proper frames, you will save yourself a lot of trouble and be much more satisfied with the final wreath. The following frames and rings represent a variety of styles, each with its own purpose.

CRINKLE-WIRE FRAMES

A single ring of heavy wire bent into a zigzag pattern, this is one of the most versatile frames for arranging fresh or dried plant materials. The zigzag form provides a grip for the wire and keeps stems from slipping as you work. This frame is the least expensive of all and can be purchased at florist shops.

DOUBLE-WIRE FRAMES

Made of four rings of wire attached in a double layer, these frames provide space for bulky items, such as pinecones, to be wedged tightly between them, forming a base upon which the rest of the wreath is built. These are used primarily for pine-cone and seedpod wreaths.

STRAW BASES

Made of tightly compacted straw wrapped with thread, these bases are popular for use with dried flowers. They create several problems. Their density makes it very difficult to push dried stems in without breakage. Also, the advantage of having a natural material for a base is lost because the thread used to wrap these bases is usually a shiny synthetic that shows through wherever the straw base shows.

The first problem can be solved by wiring dried flowers to florist picks (see Tools and Supplies, page 16) or using floral pins or wire hairpins as staples. A less expensive and more permeable substitute is a frame made of raffia (see Raffia Wreaths, p. 97).

CANE BASES

Made of round cane wound in a random design much like vine wreaths, these make good bases for decorating with ribbons and artificial flowers, as well as with dried materials. They can be painted with spray-on colors to match any decor or season.

ROPE BASES

These flat forms braided from several strands of hemp rope are very versatile. They can be decorated with dried flowers, whole spices, ribbons, and other items that are glued or tied in place with narrow ribbon. Flower stems can be tucked into the strands of the braid, concealing them and holding the flowers in place.

MOSS BASES

Gray moss provides a neutral, natural background for herb wreaths, blending well with such herbs as artemisia, lamb's ears, sage, and Sweet Annie. It is more permeable than a straw base and holds stems well.

POLYSTYRENE BASES

Never the most satisfactory of wreath bases, polystyrene tends to break apart when it has stems and florist picks pushed into it in any quantity. Molded in the shape of a wreath, it has even less stability, and because every inch of the wreath must be covered to hide the plastic, by the time it is full of material, it has often split in half—very discouraging when you've spent that much time on a wreath.

Furthermore, with the current information on polystyrene's damaging effect on the ozone layer of our atmosphere, conscientious craft workers are avoiding its use entirely.

A braided rope wreath base

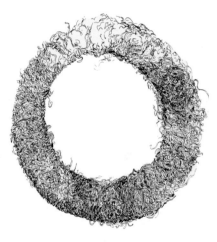

A moss wreath base

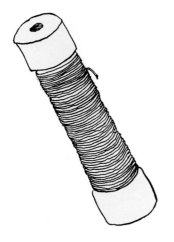

Florist wire

One of the joys of wreath making is that it requires so few tools, most of which can be found right at home. The few that you might need to buy are useful additions to the household tool drawer, handy for other craft projects as well.

WIRE

Florist wire is the best to use for wreaths, since it is available in a natural silver color, which blends well with gray herb bases, or in a dark green enamel coating, which blends with most fresh greens. It comes in a variety of gauges on spools that are easy to handle as you work. The larger the gauge number, the finer the wire. Choose a fine gauge (such as 28) that is very flexible for working with greens and herbs. Stiffer wire comes in cut lengths as well, which is handier for flower stems, since it does not have to be straightened. But for most wreath making, the finer wires are all you'll need.

FLORIST PICKS

Available in green or a natural wood color, these look like fat toothpicks with a wire tail. The wire is very fine and wraps easily around even very small stems. Picks are used to give length or strength to flower stems when they are pushed into a base. The easiest way to attach a florist pick is to hold the stem and the pick together between the thumb and first finger and roll them together. This wraps the little wire tail tightly around the stem in one quick movement. Picks are also used to combine several small flowers into a bunch, which is particularly effective on herb wreaths.

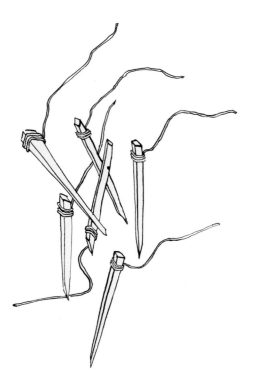

Florist picks

SCISSORS

Keep an old pair of scissors for cutting thin wires and plant stems, since this kind of use ruins good scissors. Pliers with a wire cutter can be used for stems as well as wire and should always be used for heavier wires. You may want to keep a small pair of better scissors handy for clipping threads, trimming raffia, and cutting ribbon.

ADHESIVES

In general, wreath makers use wire to attach materials. Outdoor wreaths often take a severe beating from the weather, and wire is both strong and resilient. It does not become brittle when subjected to subzero temperatures or dissolve in the rain.

There are some wreaths, however, especially those hung indoors, which require the use of glues. The craft-size glue gun can be helpful, although it cannot replace a good glue. The advantage of a glue gun is that it aims a dot of glue accurately and it dries almost instantly. Since changing humidity levels in the atmosphere cause dried material to move slightly, it is important for a glue to

remain just slightly pliable, as a glue gun does. This can be as important as the quick drying quality.

There are several disadvantages to using a glue gun. It is often awkward to use on small projects and leaves a web of little plastic strings that must be cut off. If not used carefully, it leaves behind great globs of unsightly glue on the project. Another problem with the glue gun is that it interferes with the feeling of working with natural materials. When you have a hot machine in one hand, there is a sense of immediacy and less of an opportunity to experiment, which is half the fun of making a wreath. With a glue gun, once something is in place, it's there forever.

The best glue for pinecone and dried-flower work is a thick white glue that "sets up" quickly and dries with some flexibility. Most glues and cements become brittle and cannot withstand the slight movements of dried plants as they expand and contract in response to humidity changes. Although there may be other brands that work, I have found Aleene's Tacky Glue™ to dry the fastest and clearest, and hold things in place well. In the projects, it is referred to simply as white tacky glue.

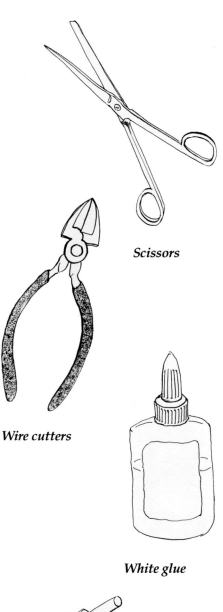

Scissors

Wire cutters

White glue

Glue gun

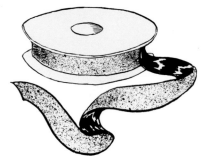

Flocked all-weather ribbon

A wire-wrapped bow

A ribbon-wrapped bow

A bow of cornhusks

Not all wreaths have bows, although there is no rule about which should and which shouldn't. There are certain kinds of bows and ribbons, however, that go best with specific kinds of wreath material. • Along with attached bows, some wreaths have wrappings of ribbon as a decoration. Compact wreaths such as those made of cane are frequently decorated this way to give them more interest. This would not work for a wreath of fresh greens or herbs. Herb wreaths, in fact, rarely have bows, which tend to clutter their simple charm.

ALL-WEATHER RIBBONS

There are several kinds of outdoor ribbon available during the Christmas season. One glossy type always looks like plastic, no matter what you do to try to disguise it. It is shiny and smooth and should be saved for use on very large wreaths hung high up on buildings, where the glossy surface is not as apparent.

Another, more attractive, option is a flocked all-weather ribbon. It is sturdy, colorfast, and holds up under the worst punishment a northern winter can offer. It is also stiff, so it holds its shape when made into large bows, and will spring back into shape even after having been weighted down with wet snow. It is a bit too stiff for making into tied bows, but works very well when fashioned into wrapped bows.

CALICO RIBBON

Available in a wide range of colors and patterns, from pale spring flowers to red-and-green Christmas motifs, calico ribbon is versatile, easy to work with, and inexpensive.

It is fairly stiff but can still be used for tied bows. Because it has plenty of body, it can be puffed out into full bows when it is wrapped with wire. Calico ribbon loses its stiffness when damp and fades badly in the sun, so it is not good for wreaths that are hung outdoors unprotected by a storm door.

Calico's "country" look makes it popular for autumn wreaths of straw and dried grasses as well as for winding around cane and vine wreaths. To use it on a miniature wreath, or to convert a wide ribbon into a narrower one, simply cut with fabric scissors; it has no selvage weave at the edge.

You can make your own calico ribbon to match curtains or other fabric in a room by spraying a length of fabric with starch and cutting it carefully with good scissors. Because calico ribbon does not have a woven edge, it frays if it is reused or if a bow has to be retied several times. If the ribbon is wide enough, however, you can iron it and trim off the frayed edges to reuse it.

SATIN RIBBON

For a touch of elegance, satin ribbon is a lovely choice. It is soft, does not have much body, and cannot be made into big bows with long loops unless it is starched first. Yet this very softness gives satin ribbon an attraction all its own. It drapes nicely, which is an advantage for more formal uses. It is not a good choice for outdoor wreaths, but its rich, deep colors make it a favorite for evergreen wreaths used indoors.

On the few occasions when you wish to add a bow to an herb wreath, satin ribbon is a good choice. Choose one of the dusty pink or mauve shades, which go so well with the gray herbs.

It comes in a greater variety of widths than any of the other ribbon choices, ranging from ¼ inch (3 mm) to 5 or 6 inches (12–15 cm). The very narrow satin ribbon is perfect for miniature wreaths, since it allows them to have bows in scale with their size. Because it unravels badly when cut, satin ribbon is not a good choice for wire-wrapped bows, but it ties beautifully, making the loveliest of real tied bows. It can also be used for elegant double or flat bows with ribbon-wrapped centers.

TAFFETA RIBBON

Stiffer than satin but not as heavy, taffeta makes beautiful formal bows. The most elegant of these are the moiré ribbons, which make crisp bows that, like calico, hold their shape without sagging. Because taffeta is not heavy, the center (the ribbon inside the knot) is tiny and tight with no bulky look. This means it doesn't have to be clipped for a wire-wrapped bow, giving it a rich fullness. It can be made into a perfect rosette bow in this way.

Also available in red plaid, this is the right ribbon for wreaths of fresh greens that are to be used in a Victorian setting.

Gingham taffeta ribbon goes nicely in a country decor and looks equally at home with straw and grasses as it does with fresh greens.

OTHER BOWS

Both raffia and cornhusks can be used to make bows for harvest wreaths and wreaths for informal settings. (For instructions on working with these, see Cornhusk and Raffia Wreaths, p. 95.)

A bright red bow, perhaps with a cluster of pinecones at its center, is the traditional accent for an evergreen wreath.

Not every ribbon is right for every type of bow. Some make lovely tied bows, others are almost impossible to tie. Some make good rosettes, others elegant draped bows. Choosing the right bow for the ribbon—or the right ribbon for the bow—is the first step in bow making. Learning the special tricks for working with each is the next step.

© William Seitz

It is easier to tie a bow around a stick or pencil.

One of the most common complaints of those who work with ribbon is the difficulty of consistently making a perfect bow. Sometimes they are straight and even, and other times they twist and turn sideways, with uneven loops and twisted ribbon. However, if you always tie the bow exactly the same way, you can be fairly sure to achieve consistent results. Try following these directions step by step, with someone reading them aloud to you as you tie the bow.

While it is possible to tie a perfect bow "in thin air" it is easier if you have first secured the center of the ribbon to something by tying it in a double knot. A pencil will do nicely. Leave two ends of equal length, allowing yourself enough for the bow itself and for generous tails. Fold the left-hand tail *under* to make the first loop. Bend this loop over, across the knot, to the right side. Leave your left index finger behind it—between it and the double knot. Your thumb is on top. Bring the right tail up and over your left thumb and the loop, under your index finger, and back through the space that your left thumb is occupying.

With your right index finger, push the loop through until it is big enough to grasp. Hold it and the center band of the bow by closing your right thumb over it. Remove your left hand and use it to grasp the loop, which is now on the left side. Pull the loop through to tighten the knot slightly.

Don't pull it tight yet, since you may want to tighten it or loosen it to make the bow even. You can move the loops and tails to make them the size you want.

When you are happy with the size and proportion, firm the knot by pulling on the *back* of the left-hand loop and the *front* of the right-hand loop. That tightens the knot without disturbing the bow at all. Slip the knot off the pencil and use the loop it forms as a base for attaching your bow to the wreath.

These may be the easiest of all bows for the beginner, because there is no tying involved. Since the ribbon is usually cut, satin ribbon is not a good choice. Taffeta ribbon, although it frays easily, can be used because it is not bulky and does not have to be clipped in the center. It pulls in quite tightly without bunching. Calico ribbon is also a good choice for these bows, as is the all-weather ribbon, which is both stiff and bulky.

Decide the width of the bow and how full you wish it to be. This method is excellent for double bows—those with more than one loop on each side— so we will begin with those. Leaving a tail the length that you wish the bow tails to be, wrap two loops of ribbon, one right over the other, making their entire span the size you wish for your finished bow. Leaving a second tail the length of the first, cut the ribbon.

Fold the looped ribbon in half in the center. With scissors, carefully cut off the corners of the center fold, removing no more than one third of the ribbon's width. If the ribbon is narrow, remove only one quarter. Repeat on the other side of the fold, as shown in the diagram.

Unfold the center, keeping the loops together. Using thin wire, securely wrap the center where the ribbon is notched using several wraps. Twist the ends together tightly and cut the wire. Carefully pull the inside loops upward and the outside loops down. Adjust the tails, and trim the ends diagonally. With a little practice you will be able to judge just how wide a bow will look right with each width of ribbon, but a good rule of thumb is that each loop should be about three times the width of the ribbon.

To make a fuller bow or a rosette, increase the number of times you wrap the ribbon. With stiff ribbons like calico and taffeta, you can make the bow three-dimensional by pulling some of the loops forward and twisting them slightly to create a half-sphere of ribbon loops.

Taffeta ribbon should not be cut in the center; the gathering under the wire will make the bow stand out and fluff even more. All-weather ribbons are quite stiff and usually quite wide, so you may have to make the notches deeper to get a nicely puffed bow. Use a slightly heavier wire for these, too.

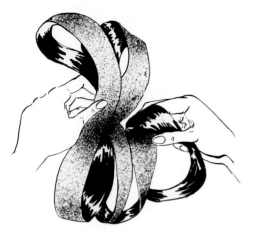

1. *Make a series of loops.*

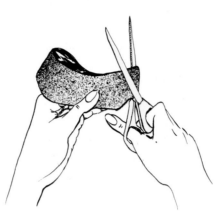

2. *Cut notches from folded ribbon.*

3. *Separate wired loops.*

4. *Completed wired bow*

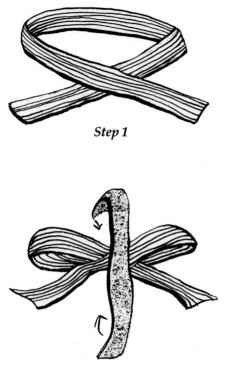

Step 1

Step 2

Sometimes you will want a formal bow with a flat ribbon band center, as though it were tied. These look like bowties and are made the same way.

Wrap the ribbon once, as you did for a wire-wrapped bow, but with a single loop on each side, and leave long tails. Fold, as you did when cutting the center of a wire-wrapped bow, but instead of cutting, place a common pin there to mark the exact center. Cut another short length of ribbon, and wrap it around the center, pinning it behind the bow. Experiment with the width of this center piece—if the full width of the ribbon seems too wide, fold the edges under until it looks in proportion. The ribbon tie at the center can be left pinned, or it can be stitched in place with needle and thread on the back of the bow. Trim ends on a diagonal.

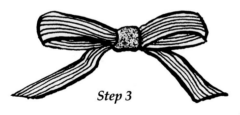

Step 3

ATTACHING BOWS

Wire-wrapped bows are easily attached to the wreath by pushing the long tails of wire through the wreath and twisting them together. For other bows, insert a wire through the back of the center and use it for tying. On wreaths with firm bases, such as commercial straw bases, attach the bow to a florist pick or put a florist pin or wire hairpin through it and push that into the wreath. On compact wreaths, such as those made of cane, you can actually tie the ribbon around the wreath before tying the bow. Tiny bows on miniature wreaths are often best attached with a drop of glue behind the knot.

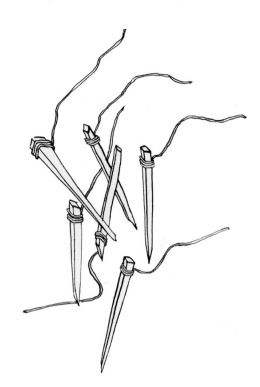

Florist picks are useful in attaching bows to wreaths.

Bow with pick attached

CHAPTER TWO

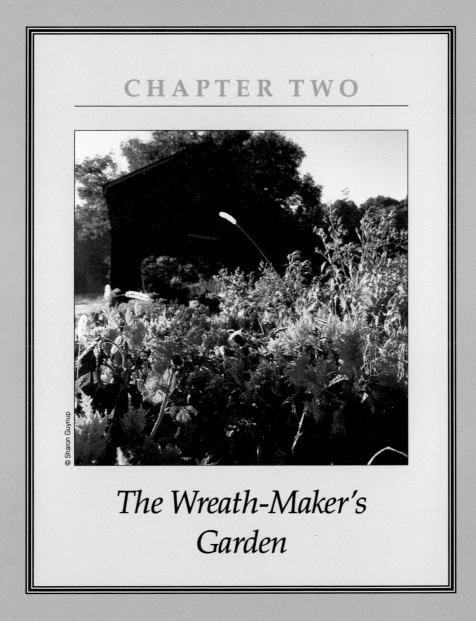

© Sharon Guynup

The Wreath-Maker's Garden

Plume celosia is an easily grown annual flower that dries to make dramatic spikes of flowers for wreaths. Globe amaranth grows in the foreground.

© Rogers Associates

If you are fortunate enough to have space for a garden and enjoy growing flowers and herbs, you can grow many of your own wreath supplies. Many of these are attractive ornamentals in the garden; some are fragrant or flavorful herbs; and a few grow in the vegetable garden. You may even want to grow a few wild "weeds," such as peppergrass, milkweed, or dock. • The lists that follow are by no means complete, but they cover some of the most commonly used and easily grown materials for wreaths.

© Robert E. Lyons

Yarrow

Achillea millefolium
(Yarrow)

The yellow varieties produce large, flat heads of tiny blossoms on plants that may grow to heights of 3 feet (1 m). Red and pink varieties have smaller flowers that grow on shorter plants. All produce mounds of fernlike foliage that spread moderately each year. A good perennial to place in the rear of a permanent flower bed. Dry by hanging in single stems.

Artemisia annua
(Sweet Annie)

This feathery annual grows tall enough that you may wish to plant it in an out-of-the-way place or as a background plant. It can easily reach 6 feet (1.8 m). Quite fragrant, it should be picked when the bead-like yellow blossoms are well-formed. Dry by hanging in large bunches.

Artemisia albula
('Silver King' or 'Silver Queen')

These tall branching perennials are used for their gray-green foliage, which makes beautiful bases for herb wreaths. They grow as high as 4 feet (1.2 m) and spread quickly from underground runners, so they are a good choice for a bed to themselves. For wreaths, artemisia should be used while it is fresh and pliable.

Plume Celosia

Celosia argentia plumosa
(Plume Celosia)

The feathery plumes come in a variety of vivid colors ranging from pale cream and yellow through deep russet orange and from pale pink through deep crimson. If the early annual flower plumes are cut off, the plants will produce subsequent crops of smaller heads on branching stems. This plant makes an attractive addition to the annual border. Dry on screens, lying on its side.

Gomphrena globosa
(Globe Amaranth)

One of the less well known everlastings, globe amaranth has an abundance of blossoms that look like compact red clover heads. They come in white, pink, and rich reddish purples and can be planted with other annuals in borders or in rows in the cutting garden. Dry by hanging in small bunches.

Gypsophila elegans
(Baby's Breath)

Great clouds of tiny white or pink blossoms turn this perennial into a white shrub when it is in full bloom. Because baby's breath may grow to 4 feet (1.2 m) it may need to be staked to prevent it from falling over, and it is usually planted at the end of a perennial bed. Hang each plant upside down and separately to dry.

Globe Amaranth

Helichrysum bracteatum
(Strawflower)

Probably the best known of all the ever-lastings, this annual has a rangy form and grows as high as 5 feet (1.5 m). Colors range from white and yellow through orange and brown and all the shades of pink and red. It is usually sold in mixed flats. Dwarf varieties are attractive in annual borders or mixed with marigolds or zinnias. Harvest by cutting each flower head individually just at its base. Place on wire stems and dry standing up in a vase or jar. The plant continues to flower until after frost.

Strawflower

Annual Statice

Limonium latifolium
(Statice)

Second only to the strawflower in popularity, this sturdy annual is available in beautiful shades of blue and purple, as well as pink, white, and yellow. Perennial forms have tiny flowers in pale lavender and white. Stems of each are quite sturdy and hold their shape when dried upright in a vase, or they can be hung in loose bundles. Either is best planted in the cutting garden.

Physalis alkenegi
(Chinese Lantern)

Be careful where you plant this sprawling plant, since it spreads quickly and invades neighboring beds. But it is well worth growing for its papery orange lanterns. Try putting this perennial in a bed of its own away from other flower gardens so that it can spread. Pick after lanterns have turned bright orange, or they will shrivel before drying. Dry by hanging in loose bunches.

Laurus nobilis
(Bay Leaves)

In far northern climates, this perennial shrub has to be grown in a pot and brought in for the winter, but it is well worth the trouble for its sturdy green leaves. For use singly and in small sprigs, press lightly after picking to prevent the leaves from curling. Use this shrub as a centerpiece in an herb garden.

Bay may be dried by pressing sprigs lightly between sheets of paper, but it is usually used fresh on a wreath and allowed to dry naturally.

Beebalm

Bay Leaves

Monarda didyma
(Beebalm)

Although the bright red and pink flowers of this perennial tea herb do not last, they are replaced by very attractive seed heads that make attractive decorations for both herb and cone wreaths. The pom-pom buttons may be as large as an inch (2.5 cm) across and are a deep brown when they have been allowed to dry on the plant. Since beebalm spreads, be sure to give it plenty of garden space.

Allium schoenoprasum
(Chives)

One of the most easily grown herbs, chives can be started from the little pots sold at the grocery store. It blooms with a pink flower that dries well and keeps its color. Clumps last for many years and may be divided to make attractive background borders. Dry the flowers by hanging in loose bunches.

Chive blossoms

Lavender

Lavandula officinalis
(Lavender)

Both the gray foliage and the spikes of tiny purple blossoms are fragrant and attractive on wreaths. Lavender's scent is one of the most enduring of the herbs. The shrubby perennial plant withstands northern winters with a little protection. In southern climates it grows into large clumps. Pick just before the flower spikes are fully bloomed and hang in loose bunches or lay in a single layer on screens.

Origanum vulgare
(Marjoram)

One of the finest herbs to grow for wreaths, marjoram has sturdy pink and magenta flowers that retain their color for years. The best blossoms come from the "wild," or "pot," marjoram, whose leaves have very little flavor. It is a hardy perennial that makes an attractive background plant. It can be dried standing in a vase.

Pot Marjoram

Rosemary

Thyme

Salvia officinalis
(Sage)

To many, this is the mainstay of the herbal wreath. Its leaves are fairly large, pebbly in texture, and a soft gray. Other varieties grow in a muted purple and in a variegated yellow-and-green combination. It is a shrubby perennial with tidy growth habits that should be cut back to only a few green leaves in the fall for more compact growth the following season. Dry as you would bay, or use fresh.

Sage

Rosmarinus officinalis
(Rosemary)

Like bay, this shrub has to be brought indoors in the northern climes. Its pine-shaped leaves dry into green sprigs that lend fragrance and texture to herb wreaths. Pinch out the tips of rosemary all summer to encourage fuller growth. Dry as you do bay leaves, or use fresh on a wreath and allow to dry in place.

Thymus vulgaris
(Thyme)

Although its leaves are small, thyme's growth is fairly dense, making it a good choice for the base of an herb wreath. A perennial, it will become a good-size bush in a few years but remain tidy and low to the ground. It keeps its shape, flavor, and fragrance when dry. Dry by hanging in loose bunches, or use fresh in wreaths.

Garlic

Zea mays
(Corn)

In addition to its contribution to the kitchen, sweet corn provides one of the finest wreath materials. Remove the inner husks carefully when you prepare the corn for cooking, and dry them on racks or screens in the sun—or lay them out on newspapers, turning them once. They become a creamy color and can be stored indefinitely.

Miniature popcorn, small varieties of Indian corn, and strawberry corn also make good wreath decorations.

Allium sativum
(Garlic)

Easy to grow from garlic cloves planted in the herb or vegetable garden, garlic bulbs make a useful and attractive addition to a kitchen wreath. Leave the long tops on when they are harvested so you will have a way to attach them to the wreath without piercing.

Capsicum frutescens
(Italian Peppers)

These hot, bright red peppers give colorful accents to an herb or culinary wreath. Their twisted shapes also contrast nicely with the textures of the herbs. Leave them on the vine until they are bright red, then string on heavy thread to dry. If frost hits before they have all turned red, dry green ones as well. They impart a good flavor to meals and, although not as good a visual highlight on a wreath, they are still attractive.

Corn

CHAPTER THREE

© William Seitz

Evergreen Wreaths

To many people, especially those who live in climates where fir and pine trees dominate the landscape, an evergreen wreath is a Christmas tradition. They hang on almost every door, and many homes have one in the window as well. If you have access to the pine or fir boughs, these wreaths are not at all difficult to make.

The favorite tree for these is balsam, not only for its pungent fragrance, which grows more intense as the season progresses, but for its rich green color, short needles, and extraordinary keeping qualities. In addition, it is often available already cut from Christmas tree sellers, who trim branches from trees or have damaged trees they must discard.

Other greens can be used as well. White pine, with its long, soft needles, makes a nice, full wreath, especially if you use a larger ring base. On very small rings, its long needles tend to fill in the center. Cedar has interesting foliage, unlike the needles of the pines and firs, and is a good green both on its own or mixed with others, where its texture makes an interesting contrast. Spruce and hemlock begin losing their needles about five minutes after they are cut from the tree. It is quite possible to end up with a circle of bare sticks after two weeks.

Scotch pine would make a good wreath, but is so stiff that it is nearly impossible to work with. Juniper can be used alone, but its needles are so short that it looks better in combination with other greens.

To gather greens in the woods (with the landowner's blessing, of course) use a pair of stout clippers or a pruning tool and cut each branch at an angle. Never strip the branches from the tree. You will soon notice, if you are gathering balsam, that the branches at the top have fuller, more three-dimensional needle growth than those at the bottom, which are fairly flat. Both are good for wreaths, but the top greens make a fuller wreath with more depth.

© Derek Fell

Cones and boughs of fir and other conifers can be turned into wreaths.

Collect the boughs into bundles and tie them near the stem end for easier carrying. Remember that the jacket and gloves you wear are very likely to get pitch on them. A layer of newspaper protects car seats from both pitch and falling needles. If you do not plan to use the boughs immediately, store them in a cool place, standing in a large bucket of water. Be sure to get them into the water as quickly as possible, before the cut ends seal over and prevent water intake. If the greens are kept standing instead of stacked, they will maintain a more natural shape. This arrangement also prevents crushing and breaking the needles.

Unused boughs should be discarded outdoors when they are no longer needed, since if left to dry out, they can become a serious fire hazard, particularly in a garage. The same is true of wreaths after they are taken down.

Opposite page: The classic holiday wreath of balsam fir welcomes guests to the Hancock Inn in Hancock, New Hampshire. This page: Cedar boughs also make fragrant green wreaths.

© Robert E. Lyons

A BASIC EVERGREEN WREATH

Evergreen wreaths are, in many places, almost synonymous with Christmas. While they can be made in any size, an 8- to 10- inch (20- to 25- cm) frame makes a good window size. The amount of greens you use determines the fullness of the finished wreath.

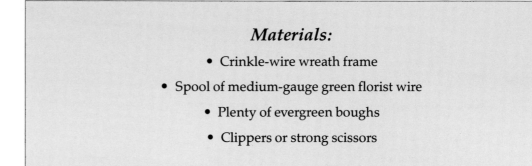

Materials:

- Crinkle-wire wreath frame
- Spool of medium-gauge green florist wire
- Plenty of evergreen boughs
- Clippers or strong scissors

Clip the tips of the boughs into sprigs, each about the same length. The larger your wreath, the longer these can be, but they should be uniform. For a small wreath, 6 to 8 inches (15 to 20 cm) is a good length. Be sure that there are no cut ends showing—all the tips should be natural ends. Assemble a large pile of these sprigs before you begin tying them into bundles. Although many wreath makers simply tie the sprigs to the wire frame without tying each bundle first, beginners will find it less time-consuming in the long run to add this step. Wrap the wire two or three times around the stems of each group of three or four sprigs, and assemble a pile of these before beginning the wreath itself. You may need to stop and make up more, which is better than making up more than you need. Begin with 30 to 50.

Lay the first bunch of greens alongside the top of the frame, stems pointing to the right (reverse this if you are left-handed). The stems should be parallel to the wire of the frame, not perpendicular to it. Tie the end of the wire to the frame securely, and begin wrapping it around the frame and the stems of the greens, using two or three wraps of wire per bunch. Add a second bunch, this time inside the frame, but with the stems still facing to the right. Again, secure with a few wraps of wire.

Continue to add bunches of greens, each one covering the wrapping on the one before it, all facing the same way, working around the frame and alternating between the inside and the outside of the frame. You may also need to place some bundles directly in the center to keep the wreath full. When you come full circle—to the place where you began—you will have to pull the ends of those first greens back and work underneath them to wire the last few bundles to the frame. Finish with several tight wraps of wire, and leave a long wire tail for a hanging loop if desired.

Look at your wreath from a distance to be sure it is even. If there are bare places, spots where the greens are a little thinner, or where the wreath is a little narrower, you can simply tuck a bundle or two of greens into the wreath where necessary, under the wire that is already there or between other stems. The shape of your wreath is determined by the length of the tips you cut. Longer ones will make larger, more open wreaths, while short ones will make narrower, more compact wreaths.

If you choose to mix the greens in your wreath, it is best to mix each little bunch. To make a double-faced wreath (one with greens on both sides), flip the wreath over after each bundle is added and wire one to the other side. Double wreaths are full and luxurious but are sometimes too thick for the space between inner door and storm door.

When you have some experience in making wreaths, you may wish to skip the step of tying the little bundles first, preferring simply to add the bunches of sprigs and tie them on with the wire. Use whichever method gives you the best finished wreath.

© William Seitz

To clean your hands after working with evergreens, use lard or kitchen shortening. These substances are much easier on your hands than turpentine or most hand cleaners, and you will not have to scrub— just rub it on and wipe it off. Then wash your hands with ordinary soap and apply hand cream.

Strings of red wooden beads combine with bright faux apples and berries to dress up a balsam wreath.

DECORATING AN EVERGREEN WREATH

A red bow is the traditional accent to finish off an evergreen wreath, but there are many other possibilities. The first is to add sprigs of other plants. For their reddish berries, select from holly, rosehips, and bittersweet. Bayberry, juniper, and mistletoe all have lovely white berries. Small, bright red apples or crab apples may be added singly or in clusters. Small pomanders tied in red gingham ribbon add fragrance as well as color, as do cinnamon sticks bundled with the same type of ribbon.

The wreath may be loosely wrapped with a garland of cranberries or popcorn. Since both cranberries and fresh apples tend to freeze if used outdoors and become soft indoors after a few weeks, they can be replaced by round, red beads or artificial apples available from florists and craft suppliers. However, the real fruit looks more natural if the wreath will not be left up for a long time.

A wreath decorated entirely with fruits, known as a Della Robbia wreath, can be made with artificial fruits or fresh ones—but the latter must be replaced as soon as they begin to look unhealthy.

Bunches of pinecones are a common accent for green wreaths. These are wired into clusters (see Cone and Seed Wreaths, page 71), then attached to the wreath with the long tails of the wire. As with any decoration, keep these clusters well balanced, but avoid a measured or entirely symmetrical look, which would be too fussy for a wild wreath.

A variety of other ornaments can decorate a wreath. Christmas ornaments, especially wooden ones, are both colorful and in keeping with the style of the wreath. Bright Christmas tree balls in small sizes can be wired to the wreath in clusters. Balls of brightly colored yarn in various sizes make unusual and attractive wreath accents. A series of yarn-covered woolly white lambs contrasts with the greens in both color and texture. There is almost no end to the decorations that look good on a green wreath, but keep in mind that the most attractive of these wreaths do not mix but rather stick to one type of ornament.

The bow can be positioned at the bottom, at the top, or even at one side, either slightly above or slightly below the center. In general, bows with long streamers are placed at the top, so the tails drape down over the wreath itself instead of trailing below it, but this, too, is a matter of taste.

© William Seitz

CHAPTER FOUR

© William Seltz

Fresh Plant Wreaths

Opposite page: Herb gardens, such as this one at Meadowbrook Farm in Pennsylvania, offer a variety of wreath-making materials, both fresh and dried.

The advantage of making wreaths from fresh plant material is its flexibility. Even herb and dried flower wreaths decorated entirely with dried materials are best created on bases made with freshly cut plants.

There are several kinds of plants that make good bases for herb wreaths. 'Silver King' and 'Silver Queen' artemisia are among the best, making firm, durable, and long-lasting wreaths of a soft gray-green color. Annual artemisia, commonly called Sweet Annie, also works well as a base, especially for herb wreaths in harvest colors with decorations of yellow, orange, and gold shades. It is more brown in coloration, and instead of leaves, is made up of tiny, beadlike flowers. It is durable and has a distinctive herb scent.

Sage, either in its more common gray-green variety or in one of the rarer purple or variegated types, makes a good wreath base, but it does have a strong scent that not everyone relishes. Its larger leaves are at their best when sprigs are used as an accent in an herb or kitchen wreath.

The sooner these herbs are used after harvesting, the better. They are the most pliable then and will shape better to the ring without snapping off. If they must be kept for a few days, stand them in a little warm water or bundle loosely and hang in a shaded place.

To prepare the plants for use, cut off the darkened, stiff bottom parts of the stems, leaving the more pliable upper stems with the best leaves as well as the flowering tips.

© Derek Fell

© Derek Fell

A FRESH ARTEMISIA WREATH BASE

One of the loveliest of all wreaths is made from dried flowers and herbs set against a base of soft, green artemisia. Its color is a particularly good background for pink and magenta flowers and herb blooms.

Opposite page: The materials for an artemisia wreath are very simple: the base wound with long stems, wire, dried artemisia, and any variety of dried flowers.

Materials:

- Crinkle-wire wreath frame
- Spool of silver medium-gauge florist wire
- Fresh Artemisia—'Silver King,' 'Silver Queen,' or Sweet Annie
- Clippers or strong scissors

Attach the end of the wire to the top of the frame by wrapping it several times. Begin with two stems of artemisia, laying them parallel to the top of the wreath frame, heads to the left, stem ends to the right. (Reverse this if you are left-handed.) About 4 or 5 inches (10 to 12 cm) from the tips, wrap the wire around the stems and the frame, securing the stems in place, but leaving the tips free. Lay another stem of artemisia over the first two, covering the wrapping, but with its tips slightly to the right of the first ones. Wrap with wire, including the stems of the first two in the wrap. Move along the frame, working to the right and bending the stems of earlier additions to the curve of the ring. As you work, be sure to cover the inside of the ring as well, using shorter tips on the inside and longer ones on the outside.

The foliage should be even and the frame covered, but the wreath does not have to be especially full at this point. You are only making a base, and it will be filled out with other material later. There is no reason why you cannot make a very full wreath at this point, but a good base is all that is necessary.

When you get back around to the place where you began attaching the artemisia, pull back their tips and work carefully underneath them to complete the base. Finish off the wreath base with several wraps of wire, and be sure to leave a long tail for a hanging loop.

To make a thicker base, or when working on a ring larger than 10 inches (25 cm), increase the amount of artemisia, beginning with three or four and adding two each time.

Hang the wreath to dry, or lay it flat with nothing on top of it until it is dry. Then it can be decorated with other dried flowers and herb blossoms. For decorating these wreaths with dried flowers and herbs, see Dried Flower and Herb Wreaths (page 103).

© Michael Grand

A LIVING WREATH OF THYME

An unusual and useful wreath, this little round herb garden gives an herbal fragrance to the table as it decorates it. While this could be hung on the wall for a few hours, it looks more at home lying flat.

Opposite page: A living wreath of thyme will last for many months if it is kept watered and gets some sunlight.

Materials:

- Double-wire wreath frame
- Sphagnum moss
- Plate with rim or shallow bowl slightly larger than wreath frame
- Rooted thyme plants

Fill the wreath frame firmly with sphagnum moss, and soak it overnight in water. Place on the plate or shallow bowl. Insert rooted thyme into the sphagnum at 3-inch (7.5-cm) intervals. For a more beautiful wreath, alternate common thyme with the lemon, silver, or golden varieties. Other herbs, such as rosemary, may be added for accent. Keep evenly moist by pouring water into the center of the dish, and add a few drops of fertilizer with each watering.

Begin this wreath when you do your final garden pruning and shaping in October so that it will be ready by Advent (four Sundays before Christmas). To add candles, simply set them in small holders in the center of the wreath and pull the herb sprigs around them. If you don't have plants that are already rooted, use soft green cuttings and dip them in root hormones before inserting them into the frame. A wreath created this way will take longer to grow lush and full. When any stem becomes straggly, simply weave it back in to cover a bare spot. Misting the wreath every week with a sprayer will keep it fresh all winter.

A LIVING WREATH OF PARTRIDGEBERRIES

Opposite page: Carefully gathered partridgeberries will take root in the moss base if kept evenly moist and out of sunlight.

This unique wreath is made of partridgeberry, a low-growing forest plant with glossy little evergreen leaves and bright red berries. Look for partridgeberry in the late fall, before snow hides it, in pine woods and low places near riverbanks. When gathering, be sure not to strip any area completely bare. Take some moist soil and pine needles from the forest floor to keep the roots damp until you can get them home. Keep the roots moist at all times, storing the plastic bag of plants in the refrigerator if you must keep them for any length of time before using them.

Materials:

- Small, double-wire wreath frame
- Sphagnum moss (about 1 quart)
- Round plate with a rim, or a shallow, flat-bottomed bowl, a little larger than the wreath frame
- Partridgeberries (12–15 long stems)

Fill the wreath frame with sphagnum moss, and wrap it with the thread or fishing line to secure moss in place. Soak it well by submerging in water for about half an hour, then lift it out and set it on the plate. Into this moss base carefully tuck the tiny roots of the partridgeberry, twining the stems along the top to cover the moss with leaves and berries. Leave the wreath in the plate of water for a few days until the plants have taken root enough to stay in place. Then lift and hang the wreath.

During the day, hang the wreath out of doors, bringing it in at night and returning it to the dish of water. A candle or a pedestal dish filled with fruit can be placed in the center.

CHAPTER FIVE

© William Seitz

Vine Wreaths

While northerners have a greater selection of evergreens to choose from for their wreath making, those living in southern climates have a wide variety of vines to work with. Along with grapevines, there are honeysuckle and a number of others from which to choose. Their flexibility and the variety of textures and colors make them especially attractive to those who prefer a wild look in their wreaths, in contrast to some of the more formal styles.

Some types of vines are more flexible than others, but all vines are at their most flexible early in the spring. Fortunately, this corresponds to the best time for pruning grapevines, so the prunings can be used for wreaths. The best way to tell if a vine is flexible enough for a wreath is to try bending it. If it is too stiff to curve in your hand, it is doubtful that any amount of soaking will soften it sufficiently for use in a wreath.

It is important to use vines as soon as possible after cutting. If you cannot make the actual wreaths quickly, at least get the vines settled into the right position by storing them coiled. An easy way to do this is to lay them, one length at a time, inside a wide bushel basket or a galvanized washtub. Any large, round container will do, but these are perfect sizes. Coil the vines one at a time so that you will be able to extract them the same way. If you put them in several at a time, they will dry together and you will have trouble separating them later.

If you do not have a basket or tub that will hold the vines until they dry, you can wrap the vines around a bucket or other round form and wire them together. After they have dried you can remove the wire, and they will hold their shape. If you wind the thickest vines around the form, you can weave the thinner, more fragile ones in and out of this base to create an interesting pattern.

If you have to cut vines in the fall when they are stiff, soak them for several days before you try to work with them, and cut only the thinnest of new growth.

© Derek Fell

Grapevines lend themselves to creating wreaths with a slightly "wilder" look.

Be careful not to knock off the tendrils, those corkscrew curls that make vine wreaths so distinctive. If you do lose one, save it and carefully glue it in place later.

Decorating a vine wreath is especially challenging, because there is no firm base to hold decorations. Everything must somehow be attached to the smooth vines, and there is no surrounding foliage to keep decorations from looking as though they had been stuck in place. Winding a ribbon around the wreath is one solution, and confining the decoration to only one area along the bottom edge is another. There it will have gravity working with it as it rests on the inside of the wreath.

Opposite page: A wreath of natural
vines is "a natural" for decorating
with a bird's nest and small birds
available at florist shops.
This page: Grapevines should be
cut in springtime if possible, when
they are at their most pliable.

© Derek Fell

A RIBBONED VINE WREATH

*The inspiration for this wreath came from a friend who found a nest of robins
hatching in a vine wreath she had hung on her front door!*

Opposite page: A tiny wreath of bleached vines can be decorated with ribbon roses in soft pastels.

Materials:

- Vine wreath
- Calico ribbon in an autumn color—1 inch (2.5 cm) wide for a small wreath, wider for a larger one, 3 or 4 times the diameter of the wreath
- Bird's nest, real or artificial
- Bird made with real feathers, available at florist suppliers, to fit the nest
- Grasses and wild seed heads, about 12 stems
- Glue gun

Wrap the ribbon in a wide spiral around the wreath, with the ends at the bottom of the wreath. Either tie them in a single bow or cut the ribbons, securing ends with a drop of glue, and cover ends with a wrapped bow (see page 18). Above the bow, set the nest and glue in place. Glue the bird to the nest. Arrange the grasses and wild seed heads around the nest in a spray, securing in place with glue.

© William Seitz

A VINE WREATH WITH FLOWERS

For this wreath, a glue gun solves the problem of getting decorations to stay on the smooth vines. Make the decorations as large and flamboyant or as spare and delicate as you wish. Try several arrangements before gluing your favorite in place.

Opposite page: A large wreath of natural vines is decorated by Chinese lanterns, bittersweet, celosia, and dried grasses, in a design created by Maria Sibley.

Materials:

- Vine wreath
- Dried Chinese lantern flowers
- Bittersweet
- Rosehips
- Dried plume celosia in reds, yellows, and oranges
- Glue gun

Lay the wreath flat on your work surface. Position the wreath so that the heaviest portion is at the lower-left-hand quarter. The bulk of the decorations are added to the upper-right-hand quarter, so this will create a balanced composition.

Arrange the Chinese lantern flowers along the upper-right area so that they lie along the wreath and extend somewhat over its sides. Place the ends of the plume celosia at either edge of the Chinese lanterns so that they follow the curve of the wreath. Add the bittersweet and rosehips to the Chinese lantern flowers in the center of the arrangment. Experiment by moving things slightly until you like the positions of all the elements, then glue them in place.

VINE TERRA-COTTA WREATH

Natural dark vines are the perfect background for this folk art wreath based on the traditional terra-cotta work of Central America. Air-drying terra-cotta clay or simple salt-dough clay can be used, or the wreath could be adorned with gingerbread figures at Christmas.

Gingerbread cookies can replace terra cotta ornaments on a natural vine wreath.

Materials:

- Terra-cotta or salt-dough clay
- Waxed paper
- Rolling pin
- Cookie cutters in flower and leaf shapes
- Cookie sheet
- Glue gun or white tacky glue

Roll dough to ¼-inch (6-mm) thickness on waxed paper, and cut designs with cookie cutters. Place on cookie sheet. If you are using salt dough, bake in 350°F (177°C) oven until well browned. Dry or bake terra-cotta clay as directed on package. When the figures are firm and dry, glue them in place around the wreath.

You can make a bow out of the dough or clay by cutting a long strip and forming the two loops, then a "knot" with another strip of clay. Set this "bow" on two additional strips to form ribbon tails, and cut the ends in a notched shape.

CHAPTER SIX

© William Seitz

Cone and Seed Wreaths

The rich shades of brown and the varied textures of cones and large seeds present a wide range of options to the wreath maker. A cone wreath can be wild and exuberant or symmetrical and restrained. It can be enormous or a perfect miniature made of tiny cones.

For those with coniferous woods nearby, the materials are free. Cones and seeds should be gathered before the fall rains and early snows have damaged them and made them hard to find. Choose a dry day following several other dry days so cones will be open and more visible. Some will be lying on the forest floor—the large cones of the white pine and the red pine, for example—while others—such as balsam and hemlock—may have to be pulled from the trees. Carry a variety of bags if you are gathering a lot of cones, so you won't have to sort them when you get home.

Look for other seeds as you go—the conelike seeds of the alder, acorns, sweet gum pods, hickorynuts, and beechnuts—as well as those on roadside weeds and in flower gardens. Black-eyed Susans shed their petals, yet their dark center cones remain, and the Siberian iris has long, dark pods that are very attractive mixed with cones. Poppies, beebalm, delphinium, baptisia, teasel, and others offer interesting shapes as well.

While it is not essential, many people are more comfortable storing these seeds and cones in their home after the collection has been baked in a slow oven to kill any insects that might harbor there. In the case of the white pine cone, which tends to be covered with spots of pitch, baking melts the pitch and make the color more even.

© Sharon Guynup

It takes a lot of cones to make a wreath—large ones for the base and smaller ones for the top.

There is little agreement with this type of wreath as to whether it is better to wire or to glue. Traditionalists use wire, but many people are perfectly happy with the glue gun. Whatever method is used, it must allow for the significant movement of the cones due to changes in humidity. Cones continually open and close enough to break the bond of glue unless it is quite flexible. If you choose a glue gun, be very careful not to leave any glue showing and to cut off all the little threads of glue that form when the gun is moved from one place to another.

Some seeds, and particularly nuts, are difficult to wire without drilling, so many people wire the basic wreath and then glue on the finishing touches and smaller pieces.

ATTACHING WIRES TO CONES

Wires for attaching cones to the wreath must be flexible enough to hide themselves inside the cones, and they should tie and twist easily. Therefore, a fairly fine wire is the best choice. Cut it in lengths of 8 and 12 inches (20 and 30 cm)—the longer ones for larger cones.

Slip the middle of a piece of wire under the top row of petals (scales) on a cone and pull it tightly. Twist the ends together securely so the wire does not slip. There should be two tails of nearly equal length. By placing the wires under the top line of petals, you can pull the tails toward the stem to attach the cone so it points directly up or leave them extending out to the side for attaching flat.

CREATING CONE FLOWERS

When cut in sections, the centers of white pine, hemlock, and balsam cones look like the spreading petals of a flower, with a small tufted center. These are not only easy to make but provide a use for damaged cones. The center of a cone is quite tough, so the best way to separate them is with the tips of garden clippers or wire cutters.

New "flowers" can be formed by gluing separate cone petals to a round seedpod center. Beebalm heads are a good choice, since they add dimension. It is easier to work with if you push the stem of the beebalm through a sheet of waxed paper and suspend it over a drinking glass. This gives you a flat base to work on but allows the stem to stay in place. Simply glue the petals around the edge of the beebalm head.

*Cut long cones into segments for
flowers.*

The cut cones look like flat flowers.

**Attach wire to the bottom or catch it
under the bottom row of "petals."**

**Additional petals can be glued in
place for a fuller flower.**

Opposite page: Cones of the white pine are large and flexible enough to make a good base for a cone wreath. This page: Spruce cones are more tightly packed than those of the white pine and make a more tailored wreath.

© Derek Fell

A CONE WREATH

The greater the variety of shapes and shades of brown, the more dramatic this wreath will look. Don't despair if you have only cones of the white pine, however; by making them into pine cone flowers and adding the tip ends for decoration, you can create an original and lovely wreath.

Nearly any coniferous forest will yield plenty of cones for the wreath maker.

Materials:

- Double-wire wreath frame
- Quantity of white pine or blue spruce cones
  (20 to 30 for a 10-inch [25-cm] frame)
- Assortment of other cones and seeds of various sizes
- Fine florist wire
- Scissors
- Glue gun

Soak the white pine or spruce cones in warm water for a few minutes until they close. Wearing gloves or using a cloth to protect your hands, push these cones between the upper and lower layers of wire on the wreath frame. You can either have them all facing out (away from the center of the wreath) or you can alternate. If they all face out, the outer edge of the wreath will be more solid looking. If you alternate, you can fill in the spaces with other cones for a less regular effect.

Allow the cones to dry overnight or put the wreath in a slow oven to dry and open. While you are doing this, wire the other cones, preparing a selection of several different kinds. Use one wire for each cone or put several of the smaller ones on a single wire. These can be the same or mixtures of different varieties.

Beginning with the larger cones, attach them along the center, covering the wires of the wreath frame completely. Push the wire tails through the wreath, and twist them together at the back, securing each cone tightly.

Don't cut these wire tails until you are finished. This allows you to find them again if you decide to rearrange the cones and also gives you spare wire with which to fasten the other cones.

One of the major advantages of the wired wreath is that you can move cones around after they are in place by simply untwisting the wires. Experiment with different arrangements of the larger cones, since these will set the tone of your wreath.

Fill in the spaces with successively smaller cones and seeds, ending with the hemlock cones and other tiny ones to fill in all the spaces where wire or frame shows. These should be glued in place by touching the stem end to the point of a hot glue gun. It is better to put the glue on the seed and then the seed on the wreath than it is to try to get a dot of hot glue into the right place.

Those who live far from pine cone country can purchase tiny cones from potpourri suppliers. To make an even smaller hemlock cone wreath, cut out a smaller circle, using a mug and a fifty-cent piece.

Materials:

- Matboard, 6 to 8 inches (15 to 20 cm) square (do not substitute cardboard, which will warp)
- Waxed paper
- Hemlock cones—about a quart
- Heavy scissors
- Glue gun
- Ribbon

Draw around a dish or a can to make a perfect circle on the board. Draw around something smaller to make the inside circle. The band of board between the drawn circles should be about 3/4 to 1 inch (2 to 2.5 cm) wide. Cut along the lines to form a ring.

Working over waxed paper and beginning at the outer edge, glue a row of cones to the edge of the ring, lying on their sides and pointing outward. Repeat on the inside edge. Then fill in the area between them, covering the cardboard base completely. You can make the center row of cones into tiny cone flowers by snipping or twisting them in half to remove the tips. Use these tips and single petals to fill in any spaces where the base shows. Glue a loop of ribbon to the back of the wreath for hanging.

AN AUSTRIAN CONE WREATH

Hemlock and other small cones and seeds combine with whole spices for a wreath in the Austrian style.

Most pine cone wreaths use a base of white pine or blue spruce cones and are at least 15 inches (37 cm) in diameter. These larger wreaths usually rely on the variety in cone shapes and seeds for their decorative interest. This traditional Austrian wreath, however, uses only very small cones packed tightly together on a compact base. To avoid monotony, they often hold highlights of bright red dried flowers and leaves.

Materials:

- Small moss wreath base, 6 to 8 inches (15 to 20 cm) in diameter
- Selection of small cones and seeds, such as hemlock and alder (about 2 quarts)
- Whole spices (nutmeg, cloves, small lengths of cinnamon stick)
- Tiny red strawflowers
- Miniature red *ruscus* leaves
- Glue gun
- Small multiloop bow made of red satin ribbon

Using the glue gun, completely cover the top and sides of the moss base with cones and seeds. Use the whole cloves as fillers to cover any moss that shows through.

When the base is covered, highlight the wreath with strawflowers and *ruscus* leaves, glued in place. Attach the bow with a dot of glue.

CHAPTER SEVEN

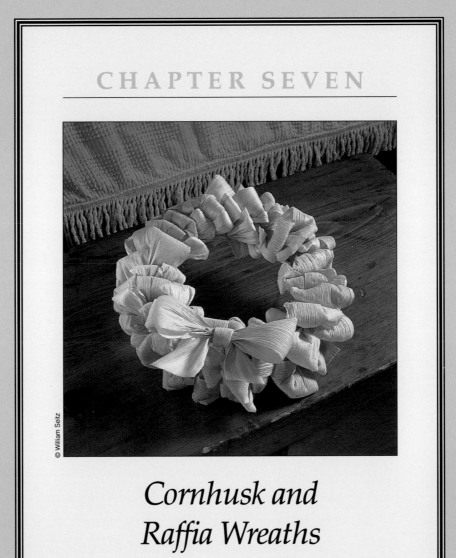

© William Seltz

Cornhusk and Raffia Wreaths

It is thought that the Native Americans taught the early settlers the beauties of cornhusks as a craft material. Coiled baskets, doormats, and dolls were created from this byproduct of table and feed corn. Later, cornhusks became a popular material for the folk arts of the peoples of southern Appalachia, where cornhusk wreaths and flowers are still made.

Raffia is made from a variety of palm, and it is valued by crafts workers for its strength, flexibility, and neutral color. Used on its own or as a binding material with cornhusks, it is a particular favorite of wreath makers.

Cornhusks cannot be used fresh from the cob, although they are quite soft and pliable then. But if used fresh, they twist into strange positions as they dry. It is important to dry the cornhusks until they are crisp and soak them until they are pliable. Afterward, they can be worked easily and will dry into the exact position they were left in.

When working with cornhusks, be sure they are crisp-dry before storing, or they are likely to mold. Husks may be dyed, and take on a lovely soft yellow color when boiled with onion skins.

Decorations made of husks can be used on cornhusk wreaths and make nice highlights for other harvest wreaths, such as those of vine or cane.

© Derek Fell

© Derek Fell

Indian corn makes a lovely and seasonal decoration for a harvest wreath.

Opposite page: A bow of cornhusks is the only decoration needed on a harvest wreath of husks. This page: A dozen ears of corn bound for the dinner table will provide plenty of husks for a wreath.

© Derek Fell

A CORNHUSK WREATH

Cornhusks are versatile plant materials that fit perfectly into informal country settings. This makes an excellent harvest wreath and will withstand sun and wind, but will deteriorate if left where it can be soaked by rain.

Materials:

- 8-inch (20-cm) crinkle-wire wreath frame
- Dried inner cornhusks—about 8 ounces (224 g)
- Several strands of heavy raffia
- Large bowl of warm water
- Red calico ribbon for bow (optional)

Soak husks in water for about ten minutes. When they soften, work with one at a time, leaving the rest in water. As the supply runs low, add more husks to the bottom.

Tie one end of the raffia to the wire frame. Take a husk from the water. If it is more than 5 inches (12.5 cm) wide, tear it in half lengthwise (it will rip like paper). Fold it in half crosswise, and gather the ends into a bundle. Be sure to leave the fold round and puffy. Lay this along the wreath frame (*not* at right angles to it), and wrap twice around the frame and base of the husk with raffia to secure. Repeat with another husk, continuing to wrap with the same length of raffia, laying the husk along the frame so that it covers the base of the first. Repeat, working along the frame so that the ties are all covered and the wreath is full with husks evenly distributed between the inner and outer edges. The back of the wreath should be fairly flat.

Continue until the wreath is full of husks. If there are bare spots when you are finished, simply tie additional husks into the spaces to fill it out. Dry the wreath thoroughly before storing, or it will mildew. Although cornhusk wreaths traditionally did not have bows, a red calico bow is appropriate.

© Michael Grand

A FRINGED CORNHUSK WREATH

A very flat wreath, this attractive decoration takes advantage of the natural tendency of cornhusks to curl slightly as they dry.

Opposite page: One of the simplest to make, a fringed cornhusk wreath takes only a few husks, and can be made from those too small for other wreaths or dolls.

Materials:

- 8-inch (20-cm) crinkle-wire wreath frame
- Cornhusks, about 25
- Scissors
- Bowl of warm water

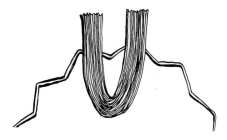

Lay folded husk strip over ring.

Soak the husks for about ten minutes to soften them. Tear husks into narrow strips. Take two of these and fold them in half together, into a U shape. Place the folded husk over the wire of the wreath frame and bring the ends up through the loop. Pull tight and turn so the ends face out away from the ring to make a fringe. Repeat this all around the ring, packing them as tightly as possible. Hang to dry, at which time the fringe will curl and give some dimension to the wreath.

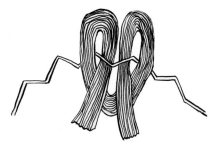

Fold ends down under the wire and pull through the loop.

Pull ends upward to tighten loop and form fringe.

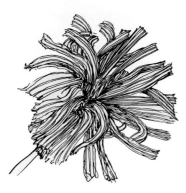

Fringed cornhusk flower

Cornhusk flower formed of petals

Flower formed of loops

Cut cornhusks into petal shapes with scissors. Gather these around the top of a natural plant stem or stiff wire to form a flower, and tie in place with raffia or fine wire. Spread the petals out until they dry, placing a crumpled sheet of paper in the center, if necessary, to keep them spread. For especially nice flowers, wire these petals of cornhusk around a natural seed head, which can form the center. Black-eyed Susan and beebalm both have neat, round heads that work perfectly.

For another type of flower, roll a 2-inch- (5-cm-) wide section of husk around a stem, and wire tightly in place. Then cut downward to make a narrow fringe. Pull these strips of husk down and outward to separate them, or spread the petals and stand the flower head down to dry.

Choose two husks of the same width, or cut two to match. Fold each in half to make loops, and arrange these like the loops of a bow, ends overlapping in the center. Wrap a strip of husk around the center where the two loops join, forming the "knot." Secure bow to a board or other surface with common pins and allow to dry. Remove pins and attach the pieces permanently with white tacky glue. (The glue will not stick properly to wet husks.) Add two tails, made from another husk, their ends cut diagonally in a notch. These bows look good on vine or cane wreaths.

Cornhusks

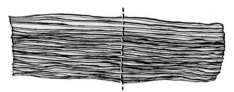

Cut into rectangles.

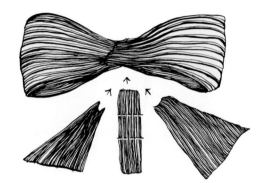

Wrap narrow strip around center and glue on tails.

Completed bow

Opposite page: Raffia is easy to braid into a wreath of any size. This page: Bright strawflowers add color to the buff tones of raffia.

© Rogers Associates

A RAFFIA WREATH

A useful material for tying other natural wreaths, raffia can itself be twisted, braided, and knotted into attractive wreaths. This one uses a simple three-strand braid and takes only a few minutes to make.

Materials:

- Bundle of long raffia strands, at least 30 inches (75 cm) long (about as much as you can hold in a circle formed between the thumb and forefinger)
- Dried grasses, herbs, or flowers for decoration (optional)
- Wide calico ribbon for bow (optional)

Without tangling the rest of the raffia, pull out two or three strands for tying. Using one, firmly tie the entire bundle together at one end. Divide into three bunches and braid firmly. As you braid, pull the bunch at the left a little tighter than the one on the right. This will cause the braid to curve slightly and eventually form a circle.

When the wreath is the proper size, or when you've almost reached the end of your raffia, cross the ends, leaving a few inches of raffia on each end. Tie the two ends together, crossing them so that the tails hang evenly. Wrap the tie over and over with raffia to secure it well and to keep the wreath in an even circle. Untie the first end, and shake loose its strands. Trim ends to match.

The wreath may be decorated with dried herbs, flowers, or grasses, either with or without a calico bow. Tiny raffia wreaths for the tree are made in the same way from just a few strands of raffia. Narrow red or green satin ribbon makes attractive bows for these.

© Michael Grand

CHAPTER EIGHT

© William Seitz

Dried Flower and Herb Wreaths

To many tastes, the loveliest of all wreaths are those made from the blossoms of everlasting flowers on a soft, muted background of dried herbs. These are year-round wreaths, with no ties to any season. They are as lovely in spring and summer as they are in the autumn, and can be made at any time.

While perennial artemisia bases are more easily made in the fall, when the stems are pliable and easily bent around the frame, they can be made from dry 'Silver King' and 'Silver Queen' as well. The annual artemisia, Sweet Annie, is easier to use after it has dried and is a bit more firm. It is used in shorter sprigs when dry, so there are no long stems to bend.

Often known as "botanical wreaths," these can also be made on a commercial straw or a raffia base, which is helpful for those without a good supply of artemisia. Nearly any dried material can decorate the wreath. Along with herbs and everlastings, you can use grasses, seedpods, and cones.

If you are growing your own herbs and everlastings for these wreaths, you should pick each just before it reaches full bloom. For flowers this means almost fully opened. Artemisia should be harvested for drying just after the little "beads" have formed in spikes along the tips. Sweet Annie should be picked when the delicate tops have turned bright yellow.

Hang flowers upside down in small, loose bunches, so they will not be crushed tightly together as they dry. Artemisia can stand in baskets to dry upright, or it can be hung upsidedown. Sweet Annie needs to be hung with the stems upward.

© Derek Fell

There is no limit to the variety of designs that can be done in dried flowers and herbs.

Hang the plants in a shaded, airy place until they are crisp-dry. They can be stored hanging as long as they are not in a dusty place, or they can be stored flat in large boxes until needed.

Dried flowers and leaves are brittle, and many of them break easily if you are not careful with them. Statice blossoms have very fragile stems just at the point where the flower joins the main stem, so be especially careful. Strawflowers that have been placed on wire stems are fairly sturdy, but the stems of most of the annuals are brittle. Work over a sheet while you are making wreaths, so you can catch broken pieces. Some of them can be glued or wired onto stems; smaller and shattered flowers can be saved for making potpourri.

While flowers dried for use in bouquets and arrangements need long stems, those used for wreaths do not. It is possible to use not only those with stems too short for arranging, but you can even use those that have broken off their stems entirely.

Even if there is a stem on the flower, it is often wiser to wire it to a florist pick, since these are stronger than the dried natural stems. Also, several flowers may be combined into little bundles for decorating a wreath. A single rosebud, for example, is lost among other flowers, but a group of three shows up nicely. By combining groups of flowers first, they are easier to attach to the wreath base. This is especially true if you are using hard straw bases.

Some flowers may present the opposite problem. Plume celosia and yarrow, for example, are frequently too large to use whole and must be broken into smaller florets. Once separated, each portion has only a tiny stem, which must be lengthened by wiring it to a florist pick.

Small sprigs of dried herbs are often wired to picks in order to keep the bunch together and strengthen the stems. Those with tiny leaves, such as thyme and savory, blend in unless they are combined into a stronger-looking clump. Others need the strength of a florist pick in order to be secured into the background material.

Those flowers that have broken from their stems entirely can be attached to florist picks by carefully running the fine wire between the petals and pulling it into the center to hide it, or the wire can be wrapped around the base of the blossom. Once these are on the wreath, they can be further secured to the background with a tiny drop of glue.

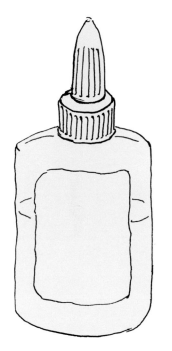

Fragile flowers may need a drop of glue on the back to strengthen them.

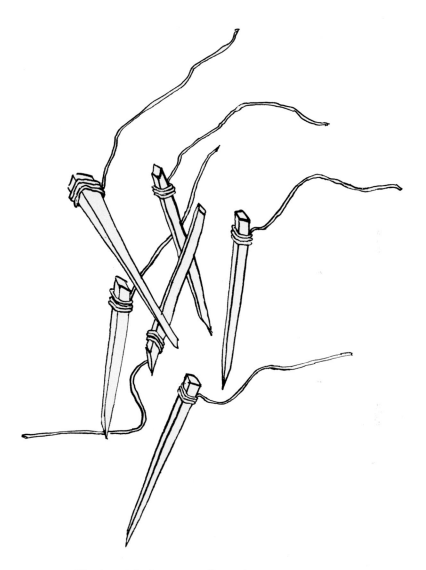

Florist picks have very fine wire attached to them.

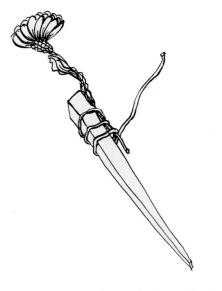

Lay the stem alongside the pick and wrap the two together with the attached wire.

A WREATH OF SWEET ANNIE AND AUTUMN FLOWERS

Opposite page: The dark brown of dried Sweet Annie sets off the brilliant color of strawflowers and the cream-colored grasses.

The soft, fragrant base of Sweet Annie provides a full background for wildflowers, grasses, and fall seed heads, with highlights of bright everlastings in autumnal tones.

Materials:

- Crinkle-wire wreath frame
- Fine-gauge florist wire, on spool
- Sweet Annie sprigs—up to 8 inches (20 cm) long
- Assortment of seed heads and grasses, milkweed pods, cornhusks, and small cones
- Yellow and orange flowers, such as plume celosia, yarrow, or strawflowers

Group the sprigs of Sweet Annie in bunches of two or three, and lay each bunch along the wire frame, wrapping the stems to the ring. Place each subsequent bunch over the wire of the preceding one to cover it, moving around the ring until the entire circle is completely covered in Sweet Annie. Be sure to keep the wreath even, laying some bunches to the outside and some to the inside of the ring to form a full wreath.

Into this firm base, push the stems of the seed heads, grasses, and other materials, taking care to keep the stems all facing the same way as the Sweet Annie stems. You should always be working in the same direction around the wreath.

After the wreath is full and balanced, add dried flowers for highlights, placing them in groups or scattering them about the wreath. Experiment until you are satisfied with the results.

Opposite page: An elegant wreath of Silver King artemisia looks even larger when hung on a round mirror. This page: Strawflowers grow in a wide variety of colors so that wreaths can be designed to match the colors of nearly any setting.

© Rogers Associates

AN EDWARDIAN WREATH OF SILVER ARTEMISIA

The delicate colors of this wreath make it perfect for a spring decoration. The soft gray-green of the artemisia is the right background for almost any color, but is especially nice with the pinks and magentas of dried marjoram flowers, globe amaranth, roses, and pink strawflowers. The darker reds of plume celosia and magenta strawflowers can be used for accent, as can the pale buffs and greens of dried grasses. Sage or lamb's ears, either fresh or dry, make a nice addition as well. The wreath can be as decorated as you like it, but should not be packed with flowers like Victorian wreaths. Its soft colors suggest a lighter, airier wreath.

Opposite page: Tiny adaptations of nearly any wreath in this book can be made for Christmas tree ornaments. Shown here are wreaths of Silver King artemisia (left), vines and cookies (lower right) and vines with a tiny bird (upper right).

Materials:

- Wreath base covered in 'Silver King' or 'Silver Queen' artemisia (this can be made as previously described with Sweet Annie or with fresh artemisia—see Fresh Plant Wreaths, page 47)

- Dried flowers in pinks and magentas, including majoram, African daisies, strawflowers, globe amaranth, baby's breath, and rosebuds

- Pale green foliage, including sage and lamb's ears (optional)

- Pinkish moiré taffeta ribbon (optional)

Working in the same direction as the artemisia, decorate the base with clusters of dried flowers. Group rosebuds together in sets of three on florist picks if they are small. Group smaller blossoms around larger ones to form accents.

You can also add accents of different pale green foliage herbs for variety, such as sage or lambs' ears, putting them directly behind the larger groupings of flowers.

Although herbal wreaths seldom have bows, this one can be decorated with a small but elegant bow of dusty pink or mauve moiré taffeta ribbon. A ribbon is not always necessary, however, especially if you use one large arrangement of flowers as an accent low on the wreath.

© William Seitz

BRAIDED HEMP KITCHEN WREATH

One of the easiest and fastest wreaths to make, this kitchen decoration takes advantage of one of the several varieties of ready-made wreath bases. The pliable hemp strands are easy to separate in order to tie spices to them.

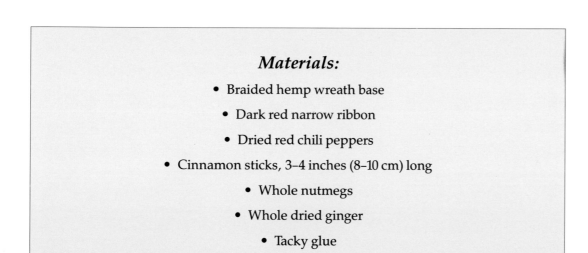

Materials:

- Braided hemp wreath base
- Dark red narrow ribbon
- Dried red chili peppers
- Cinnamon sticks, 3–4 inches (8–10 cm) long
- Whole nutmegs
- Whole dried ginger
- Tacky glue

Tie cinnamon sticks to wreath base at evenly spaced intervals. Add peppers and spices, tying or gluing them into attractive arrangements around the cinnamon sticks. Use the ribbon to accent your wreath.

Simple in construction, the grain wreath is full and fat, a symbol of the plentiful harvest. It is undecorated—no bow or other plant material breaks its symmetry. Since perfect heads of grain are hard to purchase in large enough quantity, this wreath is better chosen by someone with a field of grain at their disposal.

Opposite page: A simple circle of grain is an elegant harvest decoration for the door.

Materials:

- Double-wire wreath frame
- Raffia, 12 strands, about 30 inches (75 cm) long
- Spool of thin wire
- Large quantity of grain with perfect heads—rye, wheat, or other attractive types. A good-sized armful will make a wreath on a 10-inch (25-cm) frame, but the more, the better.

Wrap the raffia around the wreath frame to cover it completely. Working with the grain heads to the left and the stems to the right, lay bundles of grain along the wreath parallel to the frame. Secure these bundles firmly to the base by wrapping with wire. Continue adding bundles, working to the right so that the wire for each is covered by the next bunch. Keep the heads spread so that the inside and outside are full and even.

When you reach your starting point, you will have to work carefully under the first bunches to prevent breaking them. If the wreath seems uneven, you can add more heads where needed by carefully pushing the stems into the wreath. Make sure you keep all the seed heads facing in the same direction.

If you store this wreath, be sure to put it in a sealed container, since mice will be attracted to the grain.

Opposite page: *A straw base covered with miniature nosegays of dried flowers can be done in one color scheme or, as shown here, in a riot of all colors. This page: Statice provides deep blues and purples, bright yellows and almost electric pinks for wreaths.*

© Rogers Associates

A LARGE EVERLASTING WREATH

Only those with a good supply of dried flowers will want to attempt this larger wreath, since it uses a straw base that must be completely covered, instead of a base of herbal foliage. It can be made in the full palette of colors, or you can stay with one set, usually the russet tones, and highlight with others.

Opposite page: This wreath is made up of groups of dried flowers wired to florist picks, which are, in turn, pushed into the wreath base. The dried stems would not be strong enough by themselves.

Materials:

- Large straw wreath base—at least 15 inches (37 cm) in diameter
- Florist pins (sometimes called fern pins) or wire hairpins
- Large selection of dried flowers, foliage, grasses, and seed heads
- Cornhusk bow (optional)

Before beginning to attach material to the base, sort the flowers by color and size; the foliage and grasses by size. Divide each group into quarters. This will ensure that you avoid using all of one type of flower or plant on one side and help you to keep the wreath balanced.

Grouping the plants into small bundles with short stems, begin attaching them to the base with the pins, pushing them in like staples. Work on both the inner and outer edges to cover all but the very back. Use the grasses and foliage plants on the outer and inner edges, with more of the decorative flowers along the center of the base. You will find it easier to cover the inner and outer edges of each area first, then fill in the center. Once there are flowers in the center, it is more difficult to work on the edges. Some wreath makers cover the whole inside first, then the outside, completing the center afterward.

Be sure that the larger, more dramatic material is either well balanced around the wreath or grouped in a single accent design. Since these wreaths are dramatic by nature, they can be decorated with a flamboyancy not appropriate to other types of wreaths.

A single cluster of large, showy flowers, surrounded by smaller ones and tapered at the ends with long grasses, can be used as a bow, accenting one area of the wreath and providing a focal point.

A ribbon bow would be too much on this busy wreath, but if carefully planned, this is the place for a bow created of cornhusks. It should be a showy one, in rosette style, to be worthy of so commanding a wreath.

© Derek Fell

Dried Flower and Herb Wreaths • **119**

© Rogers Associates

Bundles of dried herbs on a braided raffia wreath are ready for the cook whenever they are needed. When the wreath is bare, new herbs can be added from the garden. This page: Sage leaves are larger than those of many herbs and add a soft green shade to herb wreaths.

A KITCHEN WREATH OF DRIED HERBS

While most herbal wreaths for the kitchen are made with fresh herbs that are still pliable, it is possible to create one from dried culinary herbs if they have been dried in small bundles. The greatest difficulty is in handling them gently enough that the delicate leaves will not fall off. Work over a clean cloth, and gather the leaves that drop into a savory herb blend for soups and stews.

Opposite page: Even potted herbs from windowsill gardens can provide materials for herb wreaths.

Materials:

- Loosely braided raffia wreath, no larger than 15 inches (37 cm)
- Single-wire wreath frame, the same size as the raffia wreath
- Raffia, 12 strands, about 30 inches (75 cm) long, or more shorter ones
- Small bunches of dried culinary herbs, including oregano, marjoram, sage, tarragon, rosemary, savory, thyme, bay
- Garlic bulbs
- Dried red peppers
- Bay leaves (for fresh wreath)

Lay the braided raffia wreath over the wire ring, and tie in place with a few short strands of raffia caught into the braid so they do not show from the front. This gives the wreath more strength and keeps it from losing its shape.

Tie small bunches of herbs to the front of the wreath, threading the raffia through to the back, around the ring for support, and back through to the front. Tie in bows at the stems of the herbs. Allow enough space between bunches for the herbs to be clipped for use without breaking the neighboring bundle.

In place of a bow, create an accent with garlic bulbs and red peppers, tying raffia to the stems and securing them as you did the herbs. Or accent the wreath all around with peppers and garlic.

If you are presenting this wreath as a gift, you might enclose a small pair of scissors with narrow blades to make cutting single stems of herbs easier.

If you wish to make this wreath when herbs are fresh, the best way to dry them quickly while retaining their best color is to fold each small bundle in a paper towel and dry them in the microwave oven a few bunches at a time. If you do this, you can even combine groups of herbs into small bouquet garni bundles to be removed together and used in soups and stews. Each bouquet garni should include one stem each of three or more herbs to be used together. For example, thyme, marjoram, and bay leaf make a good combination. Experiment to find others that appeal to you.

© Derek Fell

© Michael Grand

MAIL-ORDER SOURCES

Herbs, Plants, and Seeds

Goodwin Creek Gardens
P.O. Box 83
Williams, OR 97544
(503) 488-3308
plants and seeds

Gardens of the Blue Ridge
P.O. Box 10
Pineol, NC 28662
(704) 733-2417
plants

The Herb Farm
R.R. #4
Norton, New Brunswick E0G 2N0
Canada
(506) 839-2140
Catalog $5

Hilltop Herb Farm
P.O. Box 325
Romayor, TX 77368
(713) 592-5859
plants

Richters
357 Highway 47
Goodwood, ONT L0C 1A0
Canada
(416) 640-6677
seeds

Roses of Yesterday and Today
802 Brown's Valley Rd.
Watsonville, CA 95076
(408) 724-3537
rose plants

Taylor Herb Garden
1535 Lone Oak Rd.
Vista, CA 92084
(619) 727-3485
plants

Thompson & Morgan, Inc.
Box 1308
Jackson, NJ 08527
(908) 363-2225
seeds

Well-Sweep Herb Farm
317 Mt. Bethel Rd.
Port Murray, NJ 07865
(908) 852-5390
plants

Plants and seeds for drying flowers

Alberta Nurseries and Seed, Ltd.
P.O. Box 20
Bowden, Alberta T0M 0K0
Canada
(403) 224-3544

Goodwin Creek Gardens
P.O. Box 83
Williams, OR 97544
(503) 488-3308

Jackson and Perkins Co.
P.O. Box 1028
Medford, OR 97501
(800) 292-4769

Richters
357 Highway 47 Goodwood
Ontario L0C 1A0
Canada
(416) 640-6677

Shepherd's Garden Seeds
6116 Highway 9
Felton, CA 95018
(408) 335-6910

Andre Viette Farm and Nursery
Route 1, Box 16
Fishersville, VA 22939
(703) 943-2315

Wreath-making supplies and dried flowers

Christian Appalachian Project
322 Crab Orchard Rd.
Lancaster, KY 40446
(606) 792-3051

Cramer's Posy Patch
740 High Ridge Rd.
Columbia, PA 17512
(717) 684-0777

Flag Fork Herb Farm
260 Flag Fork Rd.
Frankfort, KY 40601
(502) 223-8965

Homestead Gardens
Pumpkin Hill Road
Warner, NH 03278
(603) 456-2258

A

Achillea millefolium 29

Acorns 72

Adhesives 17

Advent wreath 55

Alder 72, 83

Allium sativum 35

  schoenoprasum 33

Artemisia 29, 48, 51, 102

  albula 29

  annua 29, 48

  bases 102

Attaching bows 25

Attaching wires to cones 74

Austrian cone wreath 83

B

Baby's breath 30

Balsam 38, 72

Baptisia 72

Bases for wreaths 14

Basic evergreen wreath 41

Bay leaves 32, 122

Bee balm 32, 72

Beechnuts 72

Bittersweet 67

Black-eyed Susans 72

Bows 18ff

Braided hemp kitchen wreath 113

C

Calico ribbon 18

Cane bases 15

Capsicum frutescens 35

Cedar 38

Celosia 30, 67, 107

  argentia plumosa 30

Chinese lanterns 31, 67

Chives 33

Cleaning pitch from hands 43

Collecting greens 39

Cones 72, 102

  flowers 74

  wreaths 72, 77, 81, 83

Corn 35

Cornhusks 86, 93ff

  bow of 95

  flowers 94

  wreath 89, 93

Crinkle wire frames 14

D

Delphinium 72

Double wire frames 14

E

Edwardian artemisia wreath 109

Evergreens 41, 43, 44

  wreaths 41, 44

Everlasting flower wreath 117

F

Fir 38

Florist picks 16

Frames 14

Fringed cornhusk wreath 93

G

Garlic 35, 122

Gathering wild materials 72

Globe amaranth 30, 107

Glue 17

  gun 17

Gomphrena globosa 30

Grain wreath 115

Grapevines 60 (see also vines)

Grasses 67, 102, 107

Gypsophila elegans 30

H

Helichrysum bracteatum 31

Hemlock 38, 72, 83

Herbs 102, 121

Hickory nuts 72

Honeysuckle 60

I

Italian peppers 35

Iris, Siberian 72

J

Juniper 38

K

Kitchen wreath of dried herbs 121

L

Lambs' ears 107

Laurus nobilis 32

Lavandula officinalis 33

Lavender 33

Limonium latifolium 31

Living wreaths 55, 57

M

Marjoram 33, 107

Miniature cone wreath 81

Monarda didyma 32

Moss bases 15

O

Origanum vulgare 33

P

Partridge berries 57

Peppers, dried 122

Physalis alkenegi 31

Pine 38

Plume celosia 30

Polystyrene bases 15

Poppies 72

R

Raffia 86, 97, 102

   wreath 97

Red pine 72

Ribbons 18, 24

Ribboned vine wreath 63

Ribbon-wrapped bows 24

Rings 14

Rope bases 15

Roses 107

Rosemary 34

Rosemarinus officinalis 34

S

Sage 34, 48, 107

Salvia officinalis 34

Satin ribbon 19

Scissors 17

Scotch pine 38

Seeds 72, 102

Silver king/queen artemisia 29, 48, 102

Spruce 38

Statice 31

Straw 102

   bases 14

Strawflower 31, 109

Sweet Annie 29, 48, 102, 107

   wreath of 107

Sweet gum 72

T

Tafetta ribbon 19

Teasel 72

Thyme 34, 55

Thymus vulgaris 34

Tied bows 21

Tools and supplies 16

V

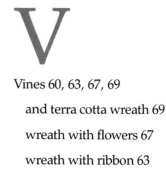

Vines 60, 63, 67, 69

   and terra cotta wreath 69

   wreath with flowers 67

   wreath with ribbon 63

W

White pine 38, 72

Wire 16, 17

   wrapped bows 22

   stems on dried plants 104

Y

Yarrow 29

Z

Zea mays 35